Reforming Bank
Capital Regulation

Reforming Bank Capital Regulation

A Proposal by the U.S. Shadow Financial Regulatory Committee

(Statement No. 160, March 2, 2000)

George G. Kaufman
Cochair
Loyola University, Chicago

Robert E. Litan
Cochair
Brookings Institution

Richard C. Aspinwall
Economic Adviser

George J. Benston
Emory University

Charles W. Calomiris
Columbia University

Franklin R. Edwards
Columbia University

Scott E. Harrington
University of South Carolina

Richard J. Herring
University of Pennsylvania

Paul M. Horvitz
University of Houston

Roberta Romano
Yale Law School

Hal S. Scott
Harvard Law School

Kenneth E. Scott
Stanford University

Peter J. Wallison
American Enterprise Institute

The AEI Press

Publisher for the American Enterprise Institute

WASHINGTON, D.C.

2000

ISBN 0-8447-7149-X

1 3 5 7 9 10 8 6 4 2

The AEI Press
Publisher for the American Enterprise Institute
1150 Seventeenth Street, N.W.
Washington, D.C. 20036

Contents

Foreword

In June 1999 the Basel Committee, which sets prudential standards for international banks, put forth a proposal for reforming bank capital standards. This monograph is the U.S. Shadow Financial Regulatory Committee's critical and constructive response to that proposal. The topic is an important one, as illustrated by the recent waves of banking crises in both developed and developing economies.

The Shadow Financial Regulatory Committee is a group of independent experts on the financial services industry and its regulatory structure.

The purposes of the committee are: first, to identify and analyze developing trends and continuing events that promise to affect the efficiency and safe operation of sectors of the financial services industry; second, to explore the spectrum of short- and long-term implications of emerging problems and policy changes; third, to help develop private, regulatory, and legislative responses to such problems that promote efficiency and safety and further the public interest; and, finally, to assess and respond to proposed and actual public policy initiatives with respect to the impact on the public interest.

The results of the committee's deliberations are intended to increase the awareness and sensitivity of members of the financial services industry, public policymakers, the communications media, and the general public to the importance and implications of current problems, events, and policy initiatives affecting the efficiency and safety of the industry and the public interest.

Members of the Shadow Financial Regulatory Committee are drawn from academic institutions and private organizations and reflect a wide range of views. The committee is independent of any of the members' affiliated institutions or of sponsoring organizations. The recommendations of the committee are its own. The only common denominators of the members are their public recognition as experts on the industry and their preferences for market solutions to problems and the minimum degree of government regulation consistent with efficiency and safety.

The American Enterprise Institute for Public Policy Research is proud to support the activities of the Shadow Financial Regulatory Committee.

CHRISTOPHER DeMUTH
President
American Enterprise Institute

Reforming Bank
Capital Regulation

Introduction and
Executive Summary

From its inception in 1986, the Shadow Financial Regulatory Committee has consistently urged financial policymakers in the United States to promote competition in the financial marketplace while ensuring the safety and soundness of depository institutions in particular. Since its founding, the SFRC has issued more than 160 statements that address those objectives. One of the themes that runs consistently through many of the statements is that sound policy requires the right blend of regulation, supervision, and market discipline to provide the proper incentives for commercial banks and thrift institutions to avoid excessive risks and to protect taxpayers, who ultimately stand behind the government funds that insure the deposits of those institutions.

In this monograph, the SFRC brings that perspective to the process of refining and extending international bank capital standards that have been in place since 1989 and that the Basel Committee on Banking Supervision—the international body of bank supervisors from the G-10 countries plus Luxembourg and Switzerland that sets those standards—proposed in June 1999 to modify.

We concentrate our analysis and recommendations on large banks—and not their holding companies—because they are the institutions that are the focus of the Basel standards and because some believe that the failure of those institutions would pose the greatest risks to the financial system. Furthermore, while we address our analysis and

1

recommendations to the Basel Committee, we believe that policymakers in the United States should adopt our proposals, whatever further actions the committee itself may take.

The standards that are the subject of this monograph—and the Basel Committee's recommendations—came into being in the late 1980s, primarily in response to concerns about the fragility of large international banks and the potential consequences of that fragility for the global economy. Those difficulties arose initially in the United States because of the less-developed-country debt crisis and later because of excessive lending for commercial real estate development. At the time, banks in the United States and some other industrialized countries already were subject to national standards governing the minimum amounts of "capital" they were required to maintain to absorb losses and, thus, to protect deposits or any entity that insured depositors from loss.[1] But because of large lending losses, it was widely perceived that many of the large international banks were too thinly capitalized.

Policymakers in the countries belonging to the Basel Committee responded in the late 1980s by setting minimum capital rules for international banks, for two reasons. First, because large international banks were active in a number of countries and were linked through payment systems and interbank deposits, regulators feared that the failure of one or more of those institutions in one country would adversely affect the financial welfare of other institutions in other countries. Second, governments of each country were reluctant to strengthen capital standards that applied only to home-country institutions because they feared that doing so would disadvantage their domestic banks when competing with banks from other countries.

The most significant feature of the Basel standards from their inception is that they have required banks to maintain more capital to support those assets or activities perceived by the committee to carry greater risks. As a result, the standards assign different assets or contingent liabilities in different risk classes or buckets, assign risk weights to those buckets, and then require banks to maintain capital equivalent to fixed percentages of their total risk-weighted assets and off-balance-sheet commitments. The general standards have continued to evolve since they were adopted in 1988, as have the capital regulations of individual countries.[2]

The Basel Committee's latest proposals for change, issued in June 1999, are the most sweeping alterations of all. In brief, the committee proposes a more refined system of risk weights and the use of ratings by private credit-rating agencies to assign risk weights to classes of assets or activities. In addition, the committee has considered permitting the banks' own internal risk-rating systems to play a greater role in determining capital requirements and has encouraged national regulators eventually to allow banks to use internal models to set their own capital standards. One of the major objectives of those proposals is to apply more market-based assessments of risk in the setting of bank capital standards.

While the Basel Committee should be applauded for seeking that objective, the SFRC believes that the June 1999 proposal is deficient in several respects. In particular, the standards erroneously continue to rely on arbitrary risk weights for computing required bank capital. In addition, the standards ignore the fact that bank risk is more properly measured by an institution's overall portfolio than by the sum of its individual assets and other off-balance-sheet commitments. The standards also distinguish improperly among different types of capital by creating two different "tiers" of required capital. Finally, the committee's latest proposals to assign assets to different risk classes on the basis of private credit-rating agencies and to rely increasingly on banks' internal models of risk are flawed in various ways that we outline in detail below.

Accordingly, the SFRC urges the Basel Committee—as well as U.S. bank regulators—to take a more direct approach to injecting greater market discipline into the setting of capital standards for large banks. Specifically, we urge the adoption of a series of independent, but mutually reinforcing, recommendations.

- The current risk-based capital requirement should be replaced by a simple, but higher, minimum leverage requirement.
- The current distinction between "tier 1" and "tier 2" capital should be eliminated. Instead, banks should be *allowed* to meet that leverage requirement with an unlimited proportion of explicitly uninsured and suitably structured ("qualifying") subordinated debentures, with the mix of debt and equity being governed by the *market* as is true for corporations generally.
- Capital should be measured by the difference between the market values of bank assets and liabilities, not their historical values.
- Large banks not only should be allowed to meet a specified proportion of their capital requirements with new issues of subordinated debentures, but should be *required* to do so—subject to certain additional restrictions that we outline further in this monograph.
- The current system of early intervention and resolution, incorporated in U.S. law by the Federal Deposit Insurance Corporation Improvement Act of 1991 (FDICIA), should be strengthened—in particular, by tying the required specific interventions to the market signals provided by the prices and yields on bank subordinated debt.

Those recommendations would apply greater market discipline to banks' risk taking and reduce burdens on bank supervisors, although supervisors still would need to determine whether banks are complying with capital requirements and to take prompt action against banks that fail to do so. A subordinated-debt requirement would achieve that objective by providing supervisors with valuable information concerning bank risk and would thereby make it more difficult for them to forbear when intervention is necessary. We emphasize that the role of supervisors continues to be important; a subordinated-debt requirement is designed to make their jobs easier and to strengthen the discipline they already provide. Moreover, a subordinated-debt requirement would provide stronger incentives for banks to disclose more information than they currently do about their portfolio risks in a timely manner to the public—and in particular to the holders of subordinated debt.

We proceed as follows. Section 1 reviews the role of capital, in theory and in practice, before the establishment of deposit insurance. Section 2 discusses the motives for regulating capital in the presence of a government safety net and reviews relevant financial history in the United States and elsewhere. Section 3 summarizes the development of international bank capital standards, their shortcomings, and the problems with the reforms that the Basel Committee proposed in June 1999. In section 4 we propose an alternative set of reforms and explain the rationale for them. Section 5 describes how our proposed subordinated-debt requirement could be implemented. We conclude in section 6.

1

Bank Capital before Federal Deposit Insurance

The primary function of capital at a bank, as at any firm, is to absorb losses. If capital is insufficient to cover losses, unsatisfied claims by depositors or other debt holders would lead to insolvency. The amount of capital that a firm maintains should be determined by, among other factors, the probability that losses of specific magnitudes will be incurred. The greater the probability of large losses, the greater should be the amount of a firm's capital in relation to its other liabilities. In the absence of government guarantees, market forces would cause a bank's capital to vary with the risk of its assets, liabilities, and off-balance-sheet positions.

The fact that capital is available to absorb losses means that it acts as a *buffer* shielding senior claimants, such as depositors or their insurers, from the risk of loss and thus enables banks to attract uninsured depositors who are averse to risk. Capital also creates the appropriate *incentives* for the firm's managers. So long as banks maintain sufficient capital, the suppliers of capital will have an incentive to limit bank risk taking, since they would bear the initial cost of negative outcomes.[3]

Before governments began protecting banks' depositors from loss, banks were subject to market discipline much like other corporations. Except for minimum capital requirements at the time a bank was chartered, the amount of its capital was determined by the market. If depositors believed that a bank had insufficient capital to

6

protect the par value of their deposits, they could withdraw their funds, frequently on demand. That threat encouraged banks to maintain sufficient capital, commensurate with their portfolio risk, to ensure the continued confidence of their depositors so as to avoid runs.

In the years before the Great Depression—or before federal deposit insurance was enacted in 1933—banks in the United States failed, on average, at about the same rate as other firms, but losses to depositors at failed banks were lower than losses to creditors of other failed companies.[4] The liquid nature of bank liabilities that allows many depositors to remove their funds immediately ("run") upon signs of financial distress, accelerated the resolution process for troubled banks and thus limited losses to depositors who did not or could not run. The smaller losses reflected the preference of bank depositors for low-risk, liquid claims—an essential and special aspect of deposits as compared with debt claims on other firms.[5] Unlike other insolvent corporations in the United States, insolvent banks were resolved not through the usual legal bankruptcy process, but instead by their chartering agencies— the Comptroller of the Currency for national banks and the state banking agencies for state-chartered banks. Market forces in the form of depositor runs—and, at times, even the prospect of depositor runs—generally caused troubled banks to suspend operations. The authorities then resolved insolvent banks relatively quickly, before they could generate additional losses, unlike the bankruptcy process for other firms.[6]

2
The Need to Regulate Bank Capital When Deposits Are Insured

Where a government safety net exists, one can no longer rely on market forces to establish the appropriate level of a bank's capital. Accordingly, in the United States, capital requirements for banks have become especially important since 1933, when the government first introduced federal deposit insurance. Initially, the insurance program covered accounts up to only $2,500. Over the following five decades, the insurance ceiling was intermittently raised, the last time being in 1980, when the coverage was lifted to $100,000, from the previous $40,000.

Even when the amount of insurance coverage is limited by law, depositors with amounts in excess of the limit may expect government protection de facto, especially if their banks are sufficiently large. In that event, it may be widely believed that policymakers fear that imposing losses on uninsured depositors at the failed bank could trigger runs by similarly situated depositors, even in healthy banks. In fact, in recent years many depositors of banks in almost all countries, including the United States, have been "bailed out" by their governments, whether or not they were legally protected by deposit insurance.[7]

In short, the central problem for bank regulation is that, although it may promote financial stability in the short run, *deposit insurance (formal or informal) provided*

by a credible government authority tends to reduce banks'
incentives to maintain adequate capital and endangers sta-
bility in the longer run. Depositors, whose accounts are
fully insured and paid promptly upon default, do not discount the gross returns offered to them by banks for the
risk that the institutions might become insolvent. Rather,
insured depositors regard their claims on banks as
riskless—equivalent to claims on the federal government—
and they discount those claims at the risk-free rate.[8]

As a result, depositors have less incentive to monitor banks' activities or to discipline banks because some
or all of their deposits are protected from loss. In turn,
protected banks face strong incentives to allow their capital ratios to fall and their portfolio risk to rise, if doing so
increases the value of the implicit safety net subsidy they
receive from not having to pay depositors to bear default
risk when the guarantee is underpriced. Deposit insurance also increases the banking system's tolerance for
incompetent and dishonest bankers, who unwittingly increase risk or operate their banks in self-serving ways,
since the insurance reduces depositors' incentives to dis-
criminate among banks according to their managers'
competence or probity.

The combination of all of the aforementioned incentives for banks to increase their risk of insolvency without
bearing the full cost of their errors—all due to deposit
insurance—is known as the *moral hazard* problem.[9] In
fact, the United States has seen many manifestations of
moral hazard in the banking industry throughout its history—even before federal deposit insurance was introduced
in 1933. Before that time, state-level deposit insurance
systems operated in some states during and immediately
after World War I. The surge in the relative prices of agricultural products during the war led some to believe—or
hope—that a permanent shift in the price of those products had occurred. Deposit insurance in the states that
offered it empowered those optimists by allowing them to

charter and operate banks and raise insured funds, which they used to supply credit for cultivating marginal lands in the expectation of high future prices. Those banks also maintained higher leverage and higher loan-to-asset ratios than were the norm for noninsured institutions. When agricultural prices declined, bank failures were widespread, and state deposit insurance funds suffered enormous losses.[10]

The problem of moral hazard resurfaced in the 1980s, when the United States experienced more bank failures than at any time since the Depression. That happened for a number of reasons. In the early part of the decade, interest rates and oil prices soared and sent the U.S. economy and other economies around the world into recession. Many large "money center" banks, in particular, suffered significant losses in their portfolios when their loans to less-developed countries proved not to be fully recoverable. Deposit insurance premiums were not increased, however, to reflect the increased risk among those institutions, nor were the banks required to recognize the full extent of their losses. As a result, certain of those weakly capitalized institutions, with the benefit of deposit insurance, took additional risks, primarily in commercial real estate lending, which later in the decade also proved to be highly costly. Other banks—many of them smaller institutions in states that did not allow their geographic diversification—suffered from a subsequent decline in oil and agricultural prices. Furthermore, the entire banking industry throughout the 1980s was subject to increasing competition from foreign banks, money market mutual funds, domestic finance companies, and domestic securities firms; that competition generally eroded banks' franchise values. The net result was a steady increase throughout the decade in the annual numbers of commercial bank failures that totaled almost 1,500—10 percent of the industry. The number of failures reached a post-Depression high of 206 in 1989, compared with an average of less than 10 per year from 1941 through 1981.[11]

The savings and loan (S&L) debacle of the 1980s is perhaps the most infamous and best-known example of how underpriced deposit insurance, in combination with regulatory forbearance from capital standards, can lead to excessive risk taking. In the absence of government deposit insurance, it is unlikely that any significant amount of short-term funds would have been placed with institutions allowed by law to operate with as little capital as 6 percent of assets but also restricted by law to investing primarily in long-term, fixed-interest obligations (mortgages). An increase in interest rates would cause the economic value of those assets to decline and, if the decline were greater than 6 percent, the corporations would be insolvent and the creditors—in this case, depositors— would incur losses. That is precisely what happened from 1979 through 1981, when a sharp increase in interest rates rendered most S&Ls economically insolvent.[12]

Nevertheless, depositors kept their funds in the S&Ls for a simple reason: deposit insurance. Depositors rightly believed that the federal government would fulfill its promises to guarantee payment of their deposits. But instead of paying off depositors of economically insolvent thrifts, regulators allowed the institutions themselves to remain in business because the losses due to the interest rate spike far exceeded the meager resources of the thrift insurance fund, the Federal Savings and Loan Insurance Corporation. In effect, Congress and the regulators gambled not only that interest rates would come down, but that the institutions would not in the meantime take additional risks. Congress and the regulators were wrong. By allowing weak and insolvent thrifts to continue oper- ating, policymakers in fact invited those institutions to assume the risk of regional recessions and even to "gamble for resurrection." When recessions occurred in the South-west and New England and a large number of the gambles for resurrection turned sour, thrift institutions suffered even deeper losses. Ultimately, in 1989, U.S. taxpayers were called on to pay substantially all the costs of removing the insolvent institutions from the financial landscape and paying off depositors—a sum that eventually totaled about $150 billion.

Of course, policymakers have long been aware of the potential and actual costs of deposit insurance. President Franklin D. Roosevelt and many others recognized the problem before federal deposit insurance was adopted. Accordingly, legislators and regulators have tried various measures through the years to limit risk taking by depository institutions.

For most of the post-Depression era, those measures have largely taken the form of restrictions on bank and thrift activities—a reflection of the implicit (if not explicit) assumption that failures are due primarily to "overbanking" or "excessive" competition. For example, after the wave of bank failures during the Depression—9,000 during the 1929 through 1933 period alone—regulators granted few new bank charters, at least until the 1960s. Interest on time-deposit accounts was subjected to a ceiling, while banks were prohibited from paying interest on demand deposits. Congress also enacted various bills designed to constrain services that banks could offer or the assets they could hold that were alleged to be—but often were not—particularly risky. Examples include the Glass-Steagall Act of 1933, which largely separated investment and commercial banking, and the Bank Holding Company Act of 1956, which severely restricted activities that could be conducted in an affiliate of a bank. Furthermore, throughout much of the twentieth century, banks and thrifts were limited in their ability to diversify their funding and lending by prohibitions on branching across state lines (and in many states, even on opening branches within the same state or county). In fact, the combination of those and other actions did reduce the number of bank failures almost to zero until the 1980s, although that result does not imply that the economy generally benefited from the combination of few failures and substantial restraints on banking.

In any event, market forces and technological advances in the 1980s and 1990s eventually induced policymakers to relax and ultimately repeal most of the Depression-era product and geographic restrictions on bank and thrift activities—a subject that is beyond the scope of this monograph.[13] In place of such restrictions, policymakers have gradually turned to *regulating bank capital* as the primary means for limiting risk taking by banks (and thrifts). That did not happen right away, however. Indeed, the initial reaction of Congress and regulators in the early 1980s to the thrift crisis was to avoid confronting the problem. As the capital accounts of S&Ls were depleted by losses from funding low-yielding mortgage loans with more costly deposits, policymakers actually *reduced* capital requirements directly by lowering the required ratio and indirectly by changing the rules governing recorded assets and liabilities.[14] In the Competitive Equality in Banking Act of 1987, Congress specifically provided "capital forbearance" for banks serving farmers that had experienced large losses.

In 1986, however, U.S. bank regulators took at least some initial steps to adopt common definitions of capital for commercial banks—and eventually their holding companies. The Federal Deposit Insurance Corporation (FDIC) and the Office of the Comptroller of the Currency moved first, followed by the Federal Reserve Board. They defined two classes of capital. Banks were required to maintain "primary capital"—shareholders' equity, perpetual preferred stock, reserves for loan and lease losses, some mandatory convertible debt, minority interests in consolidated subsidiaries, and regulatory net worth certificates—of at least 5.5 percent of total on-balance-sheet assets.

The regulators also defined "secondary capital" as including limited-life preferred stock and subordinated notes and debentures, the latter being limited to 50 percent of primary capital. Together, primary and secondary capital, or "total capital," had to equal at least 6 percent of total assets. As we discuss in the next section, the notion that not all bank capital was alike was copied in the international bank capital standards that were adopted shortly thereafter.

The common definitions of bank capital, however, did not prevent regulators (or Congress, in the case of agricultural banks) from granting troubled banks "forbearance" from meeting the capital requirements themselves. By the end of the 1980s, it was widely recognized that forbearance had contributed to the severe losses in both the banking and thrift industries. Accordingly, in 1991, Congress enacted the Federal Deposit Insurance Corporation Improvement Act, whose major objective was to *compel* bank regulators to enforce bank capital regulation. In particular, FDICIA required regulators to intervene promptly, at various stages well before a bank's capital is fully depleted, to prevent banks from taking added risks and to require them to raise additional capital.[15] The regulators were even instructed to assume control over banks that failed to comply with those requirements, before their book value equity was fully depleted.[16]

That new system of "prompt corrective action" has been a success, at least so far, although it has not been tested by such severe shocks to bank asset values as those that occurred in the 1980s.[17] Nor is the system designed to deal with fraud, which often has been responsible for substantial losses. In addition, critics question whether regulators would be able or willing officially to recognize and act upon, in a timely fashion, significant systemwide losses to capital. That concern, in part, motivates continuing efforts—including this monograph—to improve further the design of regulatory capital standards.

In sum, the clear lesson of the U.S. experience since the Depression is that, as long as the government provides deposit insurance—de jure or de facto—and bears potential losses, it must also maintain an effective system of capital regulation to limit potential losses.

The United States is not alone in that regard. Governments in other countries also offer bank safety nets and thus share the same incentive problems that our country has experienced. For example, capital-asset ratios of banks in the European Community have decreased as governments have indicated that depositors are unlikely to experience losses at failed banks.[18] Over the past twenty years, an unprecedented wave of banking system insolvencies has plagued both developed and developing countries around the globe. In several cases—including the 1990s banking collapses in Venezuela, Japan, Korea, Indonesia, Thailand, and Mexico—the estimated banking system losses have been particularly pronounced.[19]

In the process, economies have suffered two types of losses. Society as a whole loses on account of the misallocation of resources that weak and failing banks direct into unproductive investments so that through time gross domestic product declines below its potential growth rate. Furthermore, taxpayers suffer when they are saddled with the costs of paying for the cleanup of failed institutions and protecting the depositors. For example, in Japan, the world's second largest economy, the transfer costs alone have been estimated at about 15 percent of the country's GDP, and they are significantly higher in countries like Argentina, Indonesia, Korea, and Thailand, as compared with savings and loan resolution costs in the United States of about 3 percent of GDP.[20]

3

International Regulation of Capital under the Basel Standards

G iven the magnitude of past banking problems in many different countries, a key question is whether any international financial standards-setting body, such as the Basel Committee, can set standards that are adequate to the task. Nevertheless, the Basel Committee has attempted to do so, at least for the banking systems in its industrialized member countries, for a little more than a decade. We now discuss how those standards came into being, how they have been amended, what criticisms have been leveled against the standards, the most recent proposal for changing the standards, and the views of the SFRC about the Basel Committee's proposal. We ultimately conclude that the risk-weighting system that is at the heart of the standards is fundamentally flawed and may even have led to counterproductive behavior by banks that have attempted to "game" the system. As we explain at the end of this section, the most recent Basel proposal has not cured that and other problems.

The Development of the Initial Basel Standards

As U.S. bank regulators began to refine and consider tightening bank capital standards in the 1980s, they also grew concerned that unilateral increases in those standards in this country might place American banks at a competitive disadvantage relative to banks in other countries that were subject to more lenient capital rules. Special concerns were aimed at banks in Japan, which in the 1980s had grown very rapidly—along with that country's financial system—and which were then beginning to make major advances in the U.S. banking market. U.S. regulators feared that unless some attempt was made to coordinate capital standards across countries, individual countries might relax their standards as a means of enhancing the international competitive positions of their home country banks, or to protect those banks against competition by foreign banks in home markets.

There was also concern that the reliability of the global payments system—in which all international banks operated—required minimal international standards for all participating banks. In fact, the effort to establish international banking standards began shortly after the 1974 failure of the Bankhaus Herstatt, a West German bank whose unfulfilled foreign currency obligations to American and other banks caused serious dislocations in foreign exchange and international interbank markets. Consequently, in 1975 the G-10 countries plus Luxembourg and Switzerland formed the Basel Committee on Banking Supervision, whose initial mission was to develop principles for the *supervision* of internationally active banks.

The committee did not take long to focus as well on capital-adequacy standards and it thus transformed itself into a regulatory body. That happened in the 1980s, when a number of international banks suffered under the weight of nonperforming loans to less-developed countries, and prompted financial supervisors in the Basel member countries to grow increasingly concerned that further weakening in bank capital might threaten the stability of the global financial system.

While all member countries regulated the capital of their own banks, each had a different approach and definition of capital. Accordingly, the Basel Committee began in the 1980s to seek ways to promote international convergence of capital-adequacy measurement and standards, and to achieve major objectives including removing incentives for excessive risk taking by banks in their loan and securities portfolios, extending capital requirements to off-balance-sheet positions, and eliminating differences in capital as a source of competitive imbalance in banking among the Basel member countries. The committee's members believed that those goals could best be accomplished by adopting minimum capital standards for internationally active banks.

The most difficult negotiations involved the definition of *capital.* All countries regarded shareholders' equity as capital, but disagreements arose over other components of regulatory capital. The Germans regarded the broadening by the Basel Committee of any definition beyond shareholders' equity as undermining the rigor of German capital requirements. France, which had a number of state-owned banks that would have found it difficult to increase shareholders' equity, argued for including a substantial amount of subordinated debt in the definition. The United States, which had counted loan loss reserves as part of regulatory capital, argued that such a practice should be continued. The Japanese, whose banks had substantial unrealized capital gains in securities holdings, argued that such gains should be counted as assets and, hence, as higher equity.

The 1988 Basel Accord Capital Standard and Later Amendments

The resulting compromise definition—reflected in the initial standards—owed more to banks' existing circumstances than to economic logic. Specifically, the Basel Committee established two kinds of capital: core or "tier 1" capital that was mainly shareholders' equity and noncumulative perpetual preferred stock, and supplementary or "tier 2" capital that included subordinated debt (to please the French), some loan loss reserves (to please the United States), and 45 percent of unrealized capital gains on securities (to please the Japanese).

The committee also specified a risk-weighting framework to tie capital requirements to the perceived credit risks of assets and off-balance-sheet commitments. Government bonds of the countries that were members of the Organization for Economic Cooperation and Development (OECD) (which includes all members of the Basel Committee) were assigned a zero risk weight, all short-term interbank loans and all long-term interbank loans to banks headquartered in OECD countries a 20 percent risk weight, home mortgages a 50 percent risk weight, and most other loans a 100 percent risk weight. Off-balance-sheet exposures were converted into loan-equivalent values and also assigned risk weights.

The initial standards required internationally active banks to meet two minimum capital ratios, both computed as a percentage of their risk-weighted (both on- and off-balance-sheet) assets. The minimum tier 1 ratio was 4 percent of risk-weighted assets, while total capital (tiers 1 and 2) had to exceed 8 percent of risk-weighted assets. Market risks, such as interest or exchange rate risks, liquidity risks, and operational risks of banks were not addressed by the Basel standards of 1988. Those omissions were among the targets of critics of the initial standards.

In April 1993 the Basel Committee began an effort to refine the initial standards by proposing to require banks to hold capital against market risks in their "trading book"—or losses that might result from adverse changes in security, currency, and commodity prices and interest rates on securities held for sale. The required capital would be measured according to a so-called building-block approach that the European Union had adopted. Under such an approach, risks of individual types were added together and capital required against them. But several major banks found that proposal too primitive and too different from the way they managed their market risks internally.

The Basel Committee responded in a fashion unusual at the time for a body of regulators. Instead of continuing to insist on a "one-size-fits-all" standard, the committee proposed that bank capital required for market risk be based on only the supervised use of banks' internal market-risk models. That approach was adopted with the 1996 Amendment to the Capital Accord, which allows banks to use their internal models for measurement of market risk instead of the building block approach, subject to a number of qualitative and quantitative criteria, including successful back-testing of those models.

The Basel Committee has yet to institute standards for other risks—including interest rate risk in the "banking book" (primarily loans held until maturity), currency risk, liquidity risk, and operational risks—but the committee continues to search for the regulatory "holy grail." The quest not only is likely to be fruitless, but as the following review of criticisms indicates, will probably have adverse consequences.

Criticisms of the Basel Standards

The Basel standards have been subjected to a series of criticisms. We review them here, roughly in ascending order of severity.

At the simplest level, the standards have not achieved one of their central objectives: to level the playing field in banking across countries. Scott and Iwahara (1994), for example, compared the implementation of the Basel Accord in the United States and Japan and concluded that the accord had no impact on competitiveness. The authors also showed that other factors, such as taxes, accounting requirements, disclosure laws, implicit and explicit deposit guarantees, social overhead expenditures, employment restrictions, and insolvency laws, also affect the competitiveness of an institution and, in principle, its appropriate capital-asset ratio. Consequently, imposing the same capital standard on all institutions that differ with regard to those other factors is unlikely to enhance competitive equity. On the contrary, uniform capital standards may widen rather than narrow competitive differences.

The standards have also been criticized for failing to assign "correct" risk weights and for failing to promote bank safety effectively. The Basel Committee itself has recognized the validity of many of those criticisms, particularly regarding the risk weightings. As we have noted, the risk weights do not attempt to take account of market risks, liquidity risk, and operational risks that may be important sources of insolvency exposure for banks. Although the risk weights attempt to reflect credit risk, they are not based on market assessments but instead favor claims on banks headquartered in OECD countries and OECD governments, and on residential mortgages. Furthermore, the risk weights fail to distinguish among gross differences in the credit quality of borrowers within a risk class. Thus, banks engage in substantial arbitrage among loans whose risks, as determined by the market, differ from the risk weights assigned by the Basel Committee. The problems are compounded by the fact that the Basel standards are computed on the basis of book-value accounting measures of capital, not market values. Accounting practices vary significantly across the G-10 countries and often produce results that differ markedly from market assessments.

Perhaps the most fundamental problem with the current Basel standards stems from the fact that they attempt to define and measure bank portfolio risk *categorically* by placing different types of bank exposures into separate "buckets." Banks are then required to maintain minimum capital proportional to a weighted sum of the amounts of assets in the various risk buckets. That approach incorrectly assumes, however, that risks are identical within each bucket and that the overall risk of a bank's portfolio is equal to the sum of the risks across the various buckets.

Such a conception of portfolio risk bears little, if any, relation to the true portfolio risk of banks. All activities or loans within a particular category do not have the same market-based credit risk. For example, not all mortgages are exactly or even approximately half as risky as all commercial loans (reflecting the assigned risk weights), and a loan to General Electric is not as risky as a loan to Guatemala or George's Pizza Parlor. Moreover, the aggregate risk of a bank is not equal to the sum of its individual risks; diversification through the pooling of risks can significantly reduce the overall portfolio risk of a bank.[21] Indeed, a well-established principle of finance is that the combination in a single portfolio of assets with different risk characteristics can produce less overall risk than merely adding up the risks of the individual assets.

The problems inherent in assigning risk weights in the Basel standards are compounded by the inappropriate division of bank capital into different "tiers." In the process, the Basel Committee implicitly favors equity over other forms of capital—specifically, subordinated debt. As we discuss at length in section 5, the preference for equity not only is unwarranted but also may be counterproductive, since subordinated debt—which is included in tier 2 capital, but not in tier 1—often can be superior to equity from a regulatory standpoint.

Recent financial crises involving international banks have highlighted several additional weaknesses in the Basel standards that permitted, and in some cases even encouraged, excessive risk taking and misallocations of bank credit. Notably, Asian banks' short-term borrowing of foreign currencies was a major source of vulnerability in the countries most seriously affected by the Asian financial crisis. The current Basel standards contributed to that problem by assigning a relatively favorable 20 percent risk weight to short-term interbank lending—only one-fifth as large as the weight assigned to longer-term lending or to lending to most private nonbank borrowers. Putting aside the important issue of whether the standards should have assigned different risk weights for short-term lending to banks in the developed and in the developing world—a distinction not captured by the current system of weighting asset risks—it is clear that the much lower risk weight given to interbank lending than to other types of bank loans encouraged some large internationally active banks to lend too much for short durations to banks in Southeast Asia. Those banks reloaned the funds in domestic currency at substantially higher rates and assumed large foreign exchange rate risk. One would expect those distortions to be most pernicious for banks that are capital-constrained. Therefore, it is not surprising that Japanese banks, which were weakly capitalized throughout the 1990s, had accumulated the heaviest concentrations of claims on faltering Asian banks.

The current standards also assign a zero risk weight to all sovereign debt issued by countries belonging to the OECD. Although sovereign debt was not at the center of the Asian financial crises, it played a central role in the earlier Mexican financial and currency crisis of 1994–1995. Significantly, Mexico and South Korea—both of which experienced substantial bank insolvencies—are now members of the OECD; thus, the bonds issued by their governments are subject to the zero risk weight.

The last two weaknesses in particular are by now widely accepted—even among members of the Basel Committee—and have created a sense of urgency for reforming international capital standards.

The Basel Committee's Proposed Reforms: Description and Evaluation

In June 1999 the Basel Committee released and invited public comment on a proposal outlining potential improvements in its existing system of capital regulation. The SFRC has prepared this monograph in response to that invitation.

The committee proposed three important modifications to the current credit-risk standards. The first feature would require that bank loan risk weightings reflect the ratings assigned to borrowers by such private credit-rating agencies as Standard & Poor's or Moody's. As part of that first reform, the range of the risk weights was also increased (from 0 to 100 percent to 0 to 150 percent). The second element would permit banks' own internal risk-rating systems to play a greater role in determining capital requirements. The third part of the proposal contemplates extending the current "internal models" approach to market risk to setting capital requirements for the bank as a whole. The SFRC believes that all three parts of the proposal have serious defects.

The enlargement in the number of risk buckets and the link to external assessments of credit risk reflect the commendable objective of improving the measures of credit risk in bank loan portfolios. Nonetheless, the first element of the proposal entails several obvious distortions. Differences in risk weights across some risk buckets are disproportionate to credit spreads for comparably rated corporate bonds and actual historical loss experience. For example, under the proposal, loans to AA-rated corporate borrowers will require one-fifth the capital of a loan to an A-rated corporate borrower, even though the historical loss rates are quite similar. Meanwhile, variations within some risk buckets remain large relative to variations across risk buckets. A-rated companies have the same risk weight as companies rated lower, including those below investment grade (BB+ to B–), despite the fact that historical loss rates are vastly different. Finally, all unrated corporate borrowers are treated as favorably as A-rated borrowers and more favorably than borrowers rated below B–. The disparity presumably reflects an attempt to enlist support for the proposed system from countries where most firms are not rated but is unlikely to represent the true credit quality of many unrated borrowers.

Even if the proposed risk buckets were less arbitrary than the existing risk buckets, the new proposal retains the flawed summation-of-risk-buckets approach to measuring the risk of a loan portfolio. Furthermore, the larger number of risk buckets appears to confuse precision with accuracy.

The proposal to rely on ratings agencies for assigning loans to risk buckets raises additional difficulties. As Altman and Saunders (1999) have shown, ratings agencies move slowly, and changes in ratings lag changes in actual credit quality, so that the ratings have a questionable ability to predict default. Indeed, the record of the ratings agencies before the recent Asian financial crisis was particularly poor.

Furthermore, the use of private credit ratings to measure loan risk may adversely affect the quality of ratings. If regulators shift the burden of assessing the quality of bank loans to ratings agencies, those regulators risk undermining the quality of credit ratings to investors. Ratings agencies would have incentives to engage in the financial equivalent of "grade inflation" by supplying favorable ratings to banks seeking to lower their capital requirements. If the ratings agencies debase the level of ratings, while maintaining ordinal rankings of issuers' risks, the agencies may be able to avoid a loss in revenue because investors still find their ratings useful. If incumbent firms do not succumb to those added incentives, new entrants are likely to arise to meet the demands for laxity. Indeed, because entities based in the United States or the United Kingdom currently dominate the ratings business, regulatory authorities in other countries would be strongly tempted to approve new domestic ratings agencies without necessarily having full regard for the quality of their ratings. In short, if the primary constituency for new ratings is banks for regulatory purposes rather than investors, standards are likely to deteriorate.[22]

The second part of the Basel proposal, greater reliance on banks' own internal risk ratings, may be an improvement, but the current proposal raises more questions than it answers. Specifically, the proposal does not indicate how regulators will evaluate the accuracy of banks' own internal credit-risk ratings or how they would be translated into capital requirements. Nor does it explain how it would achieve comparability across the variety of internal rating systems in different banks.[23] Most important, the proposal does not explain how regulators will enforce the ratings that banks produce or impose sanctions if the ratings turn out to be inaccurate and capital is insufficient or depleted. In any event, even if an effective enforcement mechanism were in place, summing across risk buckets is just as deficient when the risk buckets are determined by internal ratings as when they are determined by external risk ratings or the current arbitrary regulatory distinctions.

Banks' own portfolio risk models solve the aggregation problem and, in principle, measure precisely the risk that should concern the regulatory authorities—the risk of loss for a bank's whole portfolio. The Basel Committee has taken note of recent advances in modeling portfolios of credit risk but has determined—correctly, in our view—that the state of the art is not sufficiently advanced to warrant relying on internal models to determine capital requirements.

Nevertheless, one could imagine a system in which regulators do not concern themselves with the validation of banks' own credit-risk models but simply require banks to commit an amount of capital to absorb all credit risks. Regulators would then levy heavy penalties on banks ex post for ex ante underestimation of their risks. That possible system has several problems, however.

One major hurdle is determining how to make any penalties *credible*. The staff at the Federal Reserve has proposed a similar "precommitment" approach for setting capital standards for market risks only. Critics have questioned whether regulators can credibly impose penalties on banks that fail to set aside sufficient capital for such risks; those critics suggest that "kicking banks when they're down" may be impractical or even counterproductive. Whatever view one takes about precommitment in the context of trading risks, the same objection should clearly apply with much greater force to any similar system for setting capital standards for bank activities *in their entirety*—or even for just the credit risks in the loan portfolio. Who pays the penalties when the bank itself is insolvent? To be sure, regulators may be able to take advantage of the prompt corrective action feature of FDICIA and assume control over an institution that has suffered large losses of capital.

Thus, it is conceivable that the gradual penalties embodied in the structured early intervention and resolution system—which we describe below—could help to make the precommitment approach, as applied to the entire bank, credible.

Nevertheless, other problems remain. Information about both the standards and bank compliance would continue to remain solely in the hands of regulators. As long as that is the case, regulators have the ability and incentive to engage in forbearance if the standards set by individual banks prove ex post to be excessively low.

Another key problem with relying on banks' internal models is the inconsistency among banks in measuring risk or even in defining such basic concepts as "default" or "loss." Furthermore, current risk-assessment models are hampered by a lack of sufficient historical data to provide reliable estimates of loan defaults. Indeed, the Basel Committee issued a report in January 2000 that

highlighted those problems and found that even sophisti-
cated banks do not express great confidence in the results their models produce.[24]

The SFRC believes that if the Basel Committee truly
wants to take advantage of market information and discipline in influencing bank behavior, it should move in a
different direction—one that relies, in part, on enforce-
able capital standards but that also makes much greater
use of the *market itself* to discipline banks against taking
excessive risks and regulators against pursuing forbearance. Below we outline such a system.

4
A Framework for Reform

The proposals we now describe have a simple set of objectives. We believe that policymakers should ensure that banks maintain sufficient capital to absorb almost all losses that they might incur. Furthermore, a mechanism must be in place that harnesses market forces so as to induce banking authorities to act promptly and effectively to bring banks into compliance with prevailing capital standards or at least to limit the losses that depositors, prudently run banks, and taxpayers may be forced to bear.

Specifically, we urge the adoption of five independent, but mutually reinforcing, recommendations. First, capital should be measured so that it substantially reflects market values and should be disclosed promptly at regular intervals. Second, banks should maintain a level of capital that is sufficient to absorb almost all losses that would be incurred by reasonably prudent management. Third, banks should be allowed to meet their capital requirements by issuing an unlimited amount of subordinated debentures—appropriately structured, among other things, to prevent banks from redeeming them before the banking authorities can act—so that the cost of capital to banks is no greater than it would be for corporations with debt that is not government-insured. Fourth, bank regulators in the United States should improve the current system of structured early intervention. Other countries that have not yet done so should adopt such a system. Finally, banking authorities should enhance market discipline on both banks and themselves by requiring large banks to issue and regularly reissue a special form of subordinated debt—a recommendation we explore in depth in section 5.

Measuring Capital

For regulatory purposes, bank capital should be the difference between the market values of assets and senior (insured) bank liabilities. Equity is the basic form of capital, but, from the standpoint of depositors, regulators, or the deposit insurer, anything that is effectively junior to their respective claims and absorbs losses serves as capital.[25] If the standard of measurement applying to assets significantly overstates their market values, the protection and incentive will be limited or illusory.

Although market valuations are not yet widely incorporated in financial reporting, the SFRC believes that reasonably close approximations to market-value accounting are feasible and relatively inexpensive for banks to adopt.[26] Unlike nonfinancial firms, banks have relatively small investments in assets for which current market values are particularly difficult to measure or estimate, such as land, buildings, equipment, work-in-process, patents, and trademarks. In contrast, most assets on banks' balance sheets can be stated at or close to their current market values.

For example, securities (including derivatives) are now stated at market values either directly or in footnotes.[27] Although most bank loans do not have readily ascertainable market values, particularly when those loans are made to small companies without publicly traded securities, a close approximation is available. After all, loan pricing reflects bank assessments using benchmarks from market yields on comparable risks. Under generally accepted accounting principles (GAAP), if correctly applied, banks are required to estimate an allowance for loan losses—a measure intended to reduce loans receivable to their net realizable value. In addition, the values of both bank loans and deposit liabilities can easily be adjusted to reflect changes in interest rates.[28]

Some other technical issues would need to be resolved if regulators were to use market values to measure bank capital. One of them relates to the fact that under GAAP, the costs of intangible assets that are developed rather than purchased (such as advertising, patents, employee training, and customer goodwill) are typically charged to expense rather than capitalized. The principal intangible assets held by banks are the core-deposit intangible and the charter value. The value of core deposits can be estimated with standard models that use the difference between a bank's deposit interest rate plus operating costs and the interest rate on purchased funds, coupled with the time pattern of deposit flows, to estimate the present value of the deposit relationship. Charter values are much more difficult to measure. For regulatory purposes, it is preferable to omit them, since the charter is likely to be essentially without value should a bank become insolvent. The equivalent loan amounts of off-balance-sheet contingent liabilities, such as loan guarantees, should also be included as assets against which regulatory capital is required, as is now done in the Basel standards.[29]

In short, a compelling case exists for regulators to measure bank capital on the basis of market rather than book values of assets and liabilities. We note that, in any event, large banks are likely on their own to improve their disclosure of useful information if required to maintain a certain amount of specially structured subordinated debt as a source of funds, as we discuss in section 5. This is so because investors whose funds cannot be withdrawn on demand and are not insured, explicitly or implicitly, are likely to demand higher interest rates on debt issued by banks that do not provide the information that enables investors adequately to assess bank risk on a timely basis. Consequently, a subordinated-debt requirement should generate added demand for and supply of meaningful accounting numbers that come closer than traditional GAAP to reporting economic values of assets, liabilities, and capital.

Minimum Required Level of Capital

Because deposit insurance greatly reduces the incentives for insured depositors to be concerned about banks' risk taking, banking regulators must require banks to operate with a sufficient amount of shareholders' capital to cover losses that banks might incur and to provide an effective incentive for banks to manage their operations in a prudent manner. We believe that the risk-weighted system of computing required bank capital should be abandoned in favor of a simple leverage ratio (which does not make use of risk weights) and that the total capital of a bank should be increased.

The Case for a Leverage Ratio. We earlier argued that the Basel standards' distinction between the two tiers of capital was driven more by the need to negotiate an international compromise than by economic logic. But that is not all. Although arguments can be made both for and against the current and proposed revised risk weights on different asset and activity categories, on balance, we believe that risk weights distort lending activity and are generally unrelated to market risk differences across and within categories of assets. Accordingly, we favor the elimination of regulatory risk weights on assets, on and off the balance sheet. The better course is for required capital to be calculated on the basis of the market values of bank assets and contingent liabilities.

To be sure, it is not obvious that uniform (and therefore, necessarily inaccurate) risk weights are less distortionary than multiple differential (and also inaccurate) risk weights. Nevertheless, a limit on leverage, without the complication of risk weighting, has the advantage of greater simplicity and is less misleading, since it does not pur-port to weigh the relative risks associated with broad cat-egories of assets. Moreover, a straightforward leverage requirement reduces banks' incentives to manipulate re-quired capital by shifting assets among risk-weight cat-egories, when those shifts do not represent real changes in portfolio risk. Nor would banks benefit from making loans to weak banks and countries simply because a lower risk factor is applied to those loans.

Of course, a single "risk" category, like a set of risk categories, gives opportunistic bankers an incentive to shift investments to assets with higher risks. For example, bankers could transform consumer loans into securitized assets by selling them to a trust and retaining a liability for the first 10 percent of loss for the pool. By doing so, bankers would retain all of the risk, but at only 10 per-cent of the capital "cost" of holding the portfolio of con-sumer loans. As we discuss next, that incentive can be diminished by a higher minimum capital requirement and substantially removed by simultaneously imposing a sys-tem of structured early intervention and resolution. In addition, large banks that meet their capital requirements with subordinated debt—especially if they are required to do so, as we propose in section 5—will have their risks continuously evaluated and priced by investors in those noninsured obligations. Thus, it is possible to prevent banks that are subject to a simple leverage requirement, without risk weighting, from engaging in activities that attempt to shift risks directly to the deposit insurance fund and taxpayers.

Raising the Minimum Capital Requirement. Currently, U.S. bank capital averages about 8 percent of (unweighted) on-balance-sheet assets, a figure considerably higher than at the beginning of the 1990s, when capital ratios were in the 6 percent range. Nevertheless, the available evidence suggests that the market would require banks to maintain even higher capital ratios in the absence of government-provided deposit insurance.

Before the creation of the Federal Deposit Insurance Corporation in 1933, capital-to-total asset ratios in the United States were about 15 percent.[30] Benink and Benston (1999) find that before the establishment of government safety nets, European Community countries had capital-to-total asset ratios ranging to about 20 percent. Kwast and Passmore (1997) show that large finance companies maintained median capital-to-asset ratios of 11 percent in 1996 and that roughly the same median ratio prevailed for the preceding decade. Smaller finance companies maintained a median ratio of nearly twice that level.

The SFRC believes that bank capital ratios should closely mimic levels that would be required in the absence of a government-provided safety net. Accordingly, we recommend that regulators raise the requirement—at least for large banks—to something on the order of 10 percent of (unweighted) on-balance-sheet assets and off-balance-sheet commitments. For example, one could use the existing Basel standards' method for computing the loan equivalents of off-balance-sheet items.[31]

Such a higher requirement need not impose any additional costs on well-run banks, however, provided that regulators adopt our view that subordinated debt count equally with equity as eligible capital.[32] Unlike dividends paid on common or preferred equity, the interest payments on debt are deductible for income tax purposes in most countries, including the United States. Treating subordinated debt as qualifying capital would put banks on a par with other corporations, which can choose the optimal mix of debt and equity on their own.

The cost of raising equity capital can also be higher than that of subordinated debt in other respects. After taking account of underwriters' fees, offering expenses, and underpricing costs of new offerings, the costs of issuing equity can exceed 10 percent of the proceeds of an equity offering.[33] Data for the period 1995–1999 show that the transaction costs of raising equity—fees plus expenses—for the very largest U.S. banks averaged 3.5 percent of their offerings. In contrast, as discussed in the appendix, underwriting costs for issuing subordinated debt, even on a frequent basis, are much smaller, even after taking into account the need to reissue debt at maturity.

Admittedly, a high minimum capital requirement would be costly to banks for which deposit insurance or other aspects of the government safety net are under-priced. But a high capital requirement and our other suggestions, if adopted, would eliminate any such subsidy—a socially desirable outcome.

Permitting Subordinated Debt to Count as Capital

The Basel standards reflect the suspicion about subordinated debt that regulators and policymakers in the member countries, including the United States, have displayed for many years. That suspicion presumably reflects the fact that debt requires the payment of interest—a contractual obligation—while equity entails no such requirement.[34] Similarly, debt principal (unlike equity capital) itself must be paid back. For those and possibly other reasons, the Basel standards assign a junior role to subordinated debt by relegating it to a second tier of capital. Even then, banks need not issue subordinated debt but instead are merely allowed to count it toward only the total capital requirement.

The suspicions about subordinated debt are ill-founded. If anything, from the perspective of both banks and regulators, subordinated debt does at least as good a job as equity of protecting depositors and the deposit insurance fund, as well as of providing incentives for banks to avoid taking excessive risks. In fact, subordinated debt offers advantages to regulators that are *superior* to common equity, in three principal respects.[35]

First, the presence of subordinated debt reduces banks' incentives to take on inappropriate risks because, for solvent banks, the incentives of the subordinated debt holders and the deposit insurance agency are aligned. Should risky activities turn out profitably, debt holders (unlike equity holders) do not benefit other than by now holding more secure obligations. But if those risks turn out badly and exceed equity, the junior debt holders bear much of the cost. Thus, subordinated debt holders, unlike insured depositors, have strong incentives to monitor and constrain banks' activities by charging interest rates that compensate them for the risks.

Second, increases in the interest yield on existing traded debt provide a warning from investors of the risks banks are taking. The ease or difficulties faced by banks in issuing new subordinated debt also provide signals about their risk profiles. Those visible market signals lead to recognition of potential bank losses, which are likely to encourage regulators and banks to manage bank risk taking appropriately and credibly.[36]

Third, bankers would have greater incentives to disclose relevant information on their risks so as to reduce the interest expense of subordinated debt. That cost would be lower, in part, because disclosure by banks would save research and analysis expenses for subordinated-debenture holders. Banks that take lower risks would benefit from effectively informing potential holders of their debentures about the favorable situation. Banks with less-favorable risk situations nevertheless would have to disclose information; if they did not, potential debenture holders would have reason to draw adverse inferences. Furthermore, once the decision has been made to disclose information about some aspect of bank performance, similar information generally will not be withheld at subsequent reporting intervals, since any interruption likely would be interpreted as an attempt to conceal a deteriorating situation.

As discussed earlier, allowing banks to count subordinated debt as capital may be financially beneficial to banks, even if they are also required to meet a higher overall capital requirement.[37] Greater flexibility in the definition of capital permits banks that legitimately wish to substitute subordinated debt for equity to do so, as that allows them to shift some of their existing uninsured debt into subordinated-debt capital to meet their minimum capital requirement.

Should regulators impose a limit on the portion of total capital that could consist of subordinated debt? To understand why the answer to the question is no, one needs simply to look to other corporations. No solvent corporation reduces its equity capital base close to zero because, other things equal, the debt holders would demand equity. The lower the fraction of equity in the overall capital structure, the more expensive debt will be, because the greater risk that the company could fail reduces the value of its debt. Accordingly, corporations choose the mix of debt and equity that they find best lowers their overall cost of capital while taking into account, among other things, the interest rates on the debt, the fact that interest is tax deductible and dividends are not, and the issuing costs of the two instruments. There is no reason for treating banks any differently.

To qualify as capital for regulatory purposes, however, subordinated debt must be available to absorb losses. Accordingly, its holders must credibly be at risk in the event of the insolvency of the bank. To perform its function, then, "qualifying" subordinated debt should have the following five properties.

First, such debt must be subordinated to all other liabilities and cannot be collateralized or convertible into equity. To ensure that subordinated debt is not bailed out (implicitly or explicitly) by the government, the deposit insurer should be prohibited by law from providing any financial assistance to the holders of that debt, even as part of a "too-big-to-fail" rescue or a "least-cost resolution." Such a requirement will prevent subordinated debt holders from seeking or receiving government protection. Similar provisions would have to be crafted for other countries, depending on their legal and regulatory structures.

Second, to count as capital, subordinated debt should have a minimum remaining maturity. The debt cannot be exchanged for other claims and cannot be redeemed before maturity except by use of the proceeds from a new debt issue of at least equal size.[38] Undercapitalized banks should not be able to redeem the debt, directly or indirectly, before regulators have the opportunity to resolve the institution, if necessary. Past experience indicates that authorities might be unwilling or unable to deal expeditiously with a bank that attempts to hide or deny its weakening economic condition. Thus, it is desirable for subordinated-debt capital to be prohibited or disabled from exiting the bank quickly. Accordingly, we assume for the purposes of this monograph that the minimum maturity on qualifying subordinated debt is one year.

Third, qualifying subordinated debt must be sold in large denominations—such as in increments in excess of $100,000 (the insurance limit for deposits)—that clearly indicate that the debt is uninsured and is specifically subordinated to the bank's other debts.

Fourth, the terms of the debt should include a covenant that permits the issuing bank, at the direction of its supervisor, to withhold payment of interest and principal if the issuing bank's capital should fall below a specified percentage of assets. Such action would become mandatory if the bank's capital ratio declined further, as is currently required by the structured early intervention and resolution requirements of FDICIA.

Fifth, qualifying subordinated debt must be sold at

arm's length to all purchasers and may not be held by or for the issuing bank.[39]

Coordination with Structured Early Intervention and Resolution

A problem to which the Basel Committee gives insufficient attention is ensuring that banking authorities act expeditiously with respect to constraining risk taking by banks that have impaired capital (or requiring them to increase capital to the required minimum). When a bank has suffered losses and might become insolvent, the authorities are often faced with strong political pressure from bankers, legislators, borrowers, and other clients of the bank to forbear from sanctioning or resolving the bank. Furthermore, equity owners of insolvent or weakly capitalized banks have strong incentives to gamble, even though the expected values of the risky investments might be negative. Those investors can lose only their investments (which are of no or relatively small market value), while they get all the gains should events turn out well.

Benston and Kaufman (1988) proposed structured early intervention and resolution to deal with that situation, elaborated in Benston et al. (1989) and further improved upon by the SFRC.[40] The United States substantially adopted that approach in 1991 as part of the prompt corrective action and least-cost resolution provisions of FDICIA. The structured early intervention and resolution system provides incentives for, and imposes requirements on, the banking authorities to act expeditiously and responsibly. If the provisions of FDICIA are enforced, especially in a regime of the higher capital requirement described earlier, the result should be almost no depositor bailouts.

FDICIA spells out five capital "zones" or "trip wires" that define first when the authorities, at their discretion, may act and when they must act.

- *Well-capitalized banks* are those with total tier 1 and tier 2 capital (or "risk-weighted capital") of at least 10 percent of risk-adjusted assets and a tier 1 leverage ratio of at least 5 percent. Conceptually, such banks are subject to minimum supervision.

- *Adequately capitalized banks* are those with total risk-weighted capital of between 8 percent and 10 percent of assets, as well as a leverage ratio falling between 4 percent and 5 percent. Such institutions are subject to more intensive regulatory supervision and more frequent monitoring, but no specific sanctions.

- *Undercapitalized banks* have total risk-weighted capital ratios of between 3 percent and 6 percent, or leverage ratios between 3 percent and 4 percent. FDICIA *requires* regulators to order those banks to develop an acceptable capital restoration plan, to limit their asset growth, and to obtain approval for any expansion of offices or lines of business.

- *Significantly undercapitalized banks* have total risk-adjusted capital ratios under 3 percent or leverage ratios below 3 percent. In such cases the regulators must require recapitalization through sale of stock or merger, restrict transactions with affiliates, and restrict deposit interest rates to prevailing levels—unless the regulator determines that such actions would not be appropriate.

- *Critically undercapitalized banks* have tangible equity capital—book value equity minus goodwill—of less than 2 percent of assets. On the presumption that those institutions are close to or at economic insolvency, FDICIA directs regulators to put them up for speedy sale or close them (with reimbursement of any net proceeds above the payment of liabilities to the shareholders), while interest payments on subordinated debt are suspended.

Assuming that regulators adhere to the requirements of FDICIA, it is unlikely that depositors would have to be "rescued" by deposit insurance, because they seldom would be at risk. The major exceptions are when capital is grossly understated, such as when a massive fraud has depleted a bank's resources, or when economic events cause a bank to suffer substantial losses before the authorities can intervene. Thus, the SFRC recommends somewhat higher capital ratios in each zone. The subordinated-debt requirement for large banks that we next describe, if enacted, would bring market forces to address all those problems more strongly, except fraud that escapes detection by investors.

5

Requiring Subordinated Debt

In the previous section we showed why it is desirable to adopt a *permissive* approach toward subordinated debt for satisfying bank capital requirements. We showed that so long as subordinated debt is of sufficient maturity and so long as the debt is strictly junior to insured deposits and to the FDIC, no reason exists to favor common or preferred equity over subordinated debt as bank capital. Subordinated debt not only provides an equivalent buffer against loss, but generally provides greater protection against the moral hazard that arises as the result of deposit insurance. Private debt holders—like the deposit insurer—suffer from increases in bank risk and, therefore, provide a source of market discipline that penalizes risk taking.

In this section we show that it is desirable to go beyond a permissive approach toward subordinated debt as a component of bank capital by *requiring* that a minimum proportion of capital take the form of subordinated debt. Furthermore, once a subordinated-debt requirement is in place, we consider ways in which market signals from the pricing of subordinated debt can be used as a regulatory tool.

Our discussion proceeds in three steps. First, we explain why a minimum subordinated debt requirement is desirable. Second, we outline the potential uses of the market price and yield of subordinated debt as a regulatory tool. Third, we detail some design features (pertaining to the frequency of primary offerings of debt and limits on the riskiness of qualifying debt) that would enhance the usefulness of subordinated-debt issues' prices as a regulatory tool. Our analysis considers the benefits and costs that arise in each of those three contexts, and we offer recommendations for maximizing the net gains of requiring and using subordinated-debt offerings in the regulatory process.

The Basic Minimum Requirement

With an appropriate closure rule and schedule of sanctions, subordinated debt discourages moral hazard problems that increase bank risk taking, especially at capital-impaired banks. Accordingly, requiring subordinated debt avoids subsidizing risk through underpriced deposit insurance. In particular, the market signals provided by the price and yield of subordinated debt not only discipline banks, but also discipline *bank regulators* by discouraging them from engaging in regulatory forbearance. Indeed, as we discuss further below, ideally, required regulatory interventions should be tied to those market signals. Furthermore, requiring a market in bank debt creates new incentives for banks to disclose information. Banks that establish credible mechanisms for increasing transparency gain through higher prices and lower yields (or interest costs) on their debt offerings.

Accordingly, we propose that large banks be required to back at least 2 percent of their outstanding assets and off-balance-sheet commitments with subordinated debt that meets the five criteria outlined in the previous section. That is, qualifying subordinated debt would be of a minimum remaining maturity (say, one year), would be held at arm's length, and could not be repaid by the government or the FDIC. In particular, as argued above, to ensure that subordinated debt is really junior to deposits, it could not be collateralized, there should be a prohibition on its repayment in the event other uninsured debts are protected by the FDIC either as part of a "least-cost resolution" or a "too-big-to-fail" intervention, and regulators should have the power and the mandate to withhold interest and principal payments in accordance with the rules under structured early intervention and resolution.

How large must a bank be to be subject to the requirement? In large part, that depends on the costs of issuing debt for banks of different sizes that in turn depend heavily on the depth of the market. Initially, we propose that the requirement apply to banks with assets greater than $10 billion, a threshold that would cover roughly two-thirds of the assets in the U.S. banking system.[41] Banks with assets of $10 billion or more should be able to place their debt in public or private markets at reasonable cost. Over time, as transaction costs come down and the subordinated debt market deepens, regulators can and should consider lowering the size threshold for the requirement—or, at the very least, not adjusting it for inflation (which would have the effect of lowering it in real terms).[42]

Who should issue subordinated debt, banks or their holding companies? To answer that question one must begin with the broader question of whether chartered banks or their holding companies are the targets of prudential bank regulation. The Shadow Financial Regulatory Committee has argued on several occasions[43] that the insured bank, and not its holding company, should be the entity controlled by prudential regulation.[44] The primary goal of prudential regulation is to prevent abuse of the safety net. A secondary goal is to prevent disruptions in the payments system. Both those goals point clearly to commercial banks as the appropriate entities to which prudential regulation, including capital and subordinated-debt requirements, should be applied.

What effect would that narrow focus for prudential regulation have on incentives for risk shifting between nonbank and bank affiliates within holding companies?

Are existing "firewalls" adequate to limit risk shifting? The primary firewalls that limit the ability of nonbanks to transfer risk to their bank affiliates are the restrictions on lending or guarantees by banks to affiliates—sections 23A and 23B of the Federal Reserve Act—and limitations on bank dividend payments to the holding company to constrain the possibility of transfers of capital from banks to nonbanks. Violations of those constraints are rare. One could argue that imposing a perfectly functioning subordinated-debt requirement on chartered banks would obviate the need for any additional measures, since banks would be penalized by the market for any attempted risk shifting from the holding company to the bank. But we do not envision that it would be possible to create so perfect a subordinated-debt regime, and therefore we recommend retaining existing firewalls as an additional safeguard.

To be effective, the 2 percent minimum requirement must be enforced. Regulators would be required to monitor compliance with the rule (which is easy to ascertain). Any bank found in violation would immediately receive notice of the violation and, if necessary, a cease-and-desist order and could be penalized for failing to comply with that notice in a timely manner (even if the bank was otherwise in compliance with other regulations, including total capital requirements). Regulatory sanctions for failure to comply with the subordinated-debt requirement—such as suspension of dividends, limits on growth, and the like—must be set according to clear rules and should not be a matter of regulators' discretion. Those sanctions should be integrated with the sanctions in the structured early intervention and resolution system, such as that mandated by FDICIA in the United States. Moreover, regulators must enforce a closure rule that requires timely resolution when a bank's equity declines to 2 percent of its assets; for subordinated debt to maintain its favorable risk characteristics relative to equity, it cannot be permitted to become, in effect, a form of equity.

Part of the advantage of a subordinated-debt requirement is that, if enforced, it would provide an automatic
source of market discipline over banks that also acts as a
check against regulatory forbearance. Banks that maintain high default risk will find it harder to place subordinated debt at low cost. Not only will their costs of funds
rise, but at high levels of risk banks may be rationed out
of the subordinated-debt market for reasons elaborated
by Stiglitz and Weiss (1981). The retirement of subordinated debt as it matures, if not replaced, would force
shrinkage of assets to reduce risks to subordinated-debt
holders. But such a market mechanism can work only if
regulators can be depended upon to enforce compliance
with the minimum requirement—hence the need for clear
rules that make enforcement credible.

It is worth emphasizing that, as a disciplinary device, subordinated debt is somewhat different from uninsured demandable debt—primarily deposits—for two
reasons. First, subordinated debt is junior to deposits and
general creditors both because of its legal status and because it cannot be repaid as quickly and thus is riskier.
The greater risk of subordinated debt motivates more
monitoring effort on the part of subordinated debt holders, and because subordinated debt buffers the risk of
other debts, its existence will concentrate monitoring efforts in the hands of subordinated debt holders. Second,
qualifying subordinated debt cannot be put back to the
issuer, but instead matures over time. Therefore, if a bank
faces a sudden problem, subordinated-debt withdrawals
will not be as rapid as deposit runs have been in the past.
Thus, discipline will be applied on a continuing basis rather
than suddenly and at one time.[45]

These two differences—that "runs" by subordinated
debt holders will necessarily be more gradual than runs
by depositors and that monitoring will be more concen-
trated in fewer hands—have a positive and a negative side.
On the positive side, concentration of monitoring and

gradual discipline may reduce total monitoring costs and lower liquidity risk. Furthermore, gradual discipline makes it less likely that government authorities will use a "liquidity crisis" as an excuse to subvert market discipline through intervention to assist banks suffering withdrawals. On the negative side, the gradual withdrawal of subordinated debt is not as powerful a disciplinary force as the rapid contraction of demandable deposits. That suggests that for subordinated debt to be a fully effective disciplinary device, regulators must reinforce the market signals and gradual shrinkage of subordinated debt outstanding with regulatory interventions, which we discuss below.

Finally, requiring the use of subordinated debt could entail costs as well as benefits. Would a mandatory subordinated-debt requirement impose new transaction costs associated with debt offerings? Probably not. Equity also has issuing costs, which are higher but occur only at the initial offering date. In contrast to equity, subordinated debt matures and must be rolled over periodically. Nevertheless, as explained in greater detail in the appendix, even taking into account the costs of recurrent issues of subordinated debt, it is highly unlikely that the annualized issuing costs of subordinated debt would be as high as those of equity.

It is important to recognize, however, that equity capital can be built up through retained earnings, rather than by issuing stock. Raising equity capital internally—for example, by reducing dividends—is less expensive than issuing new shares. Thus, if equity is obtained through a mix of new offerings and the accumulation of retained earnings, it is conceivable that the issuing costs of subordinated debt make it a more costly alternative to equity. Yet, even in such a case, the relative transaction cost of meeting a 2 percent subordinated-debt requirement should still have a very small effect on bank profit.

Might a subordinated-debt requirement raise a bank's

leverage ratio above its optimal level? We believe that such an outcome is unlikely for two reasons. First, total bank debt consists of deposits as well as subordinated debt. Banks wishing to maintain any given leverage ratio could easily do so by reducing their deposits or other debt outstanding by the amount of their new subordinated-debt offerings. Second, because subordinated debt would create new incentives to limit bank risk, it likely would produce both *lower* asset risk and *lower* leverage. That outcome is especially likely if—as we suggest below—the risk of subordinated debt were limited by additional regulatory restrictions. In short, subordinated debt is likely to raise the equity ratios of banks, not lower them. Holders of subordinated debt would demand a sufficient buffer of capital junior to them.

That possibility raises a potential opposite objection to a subordinated-debt requirement: that it would raise banks' costs unnecessarily by forcing banks to increase their equity-to-debt ratios (which would increase tax and underwriting costs). While it is likely that a requirement of the kind we are proposing would, in fact, raise banks' desired equity ratios, it would not raise them *unnecessarily*. A bank that holds adequate capital and maintains asset risk levels consistent with prudent risk management will not be forced to raise its equity capital ratio by the new subordinated-debt requirement. Only banks operating with imprudently low capital ratios before the imposition of the requirement will find it a binding constraint, and for those banks the increase in equity capital is desirable.

Using Price Signals from Subordinated Debt in the Regulatory Process

So far, we have shown how a subordinated-debt requirement can act as an independent source of market monitoring and discipline over banks to constrain their risk of insolvency. But regulators could and should use the signals produced by the price subordinated debt commands in the market to augment the information they collect as part of their regular examinations of banks and to spur, and at times require, regulatory interventions.

How would the price and yield signals be used? Several possibilities exist. A minimal approach would require that the signals be disclosed on a continuing basis to regulators, to be used as the regulators see fit. Market prices and yields also could and should be among the many pieces of information for determining deposit insurance premiums and the frequency of supervisory examinations.

A more ambitious approach, and one that the SFRC endorses, is that regulators be required to establish more formal guidelines—which are integrated with the sanctions schedule set forth in FDICIA—for incorporating market signals into the regulatory process. For example, a bank whose debt yields rise to "junk" levels—say, above the prevailing premium of interest rates on BBB-rated securities relative to Treasury securities of comparable maturity—should automatically face an examination, pay a higher level of premiums for deposit insurance, and be placed in the category of undercapitalized institutions. That would require the bank to devise a strategy for improving its position and the market's perception of its riskiness and would subject it to restrictions on the interest rates it could pay depositors, the dividends it could pay to shareholders, and asset growth.

There are at least two benefits of establishing clear rules for the regulatory use of market signals provided by subordinated debt. First, clear rules constrain undesirable forbearance by regulators. Second, regulatory behavior would be more predictable, thereby reducing banks' regulatory risk and enhancing fair treatment of all banks. There is a cost, though, in that market prices may provide false signals of bank quality that result in misguided regulatory actions.

Thus, the use of market prices as a regulatory tool will only be desirable if the prices and yields of the debt instruments reflect information about the banks that issue them. That consideration suggests that it may be desirable to regulate the process of issuing debt in a way that ensures a steady flow of high-quality information to regulators to ensure that they need not rely on isolated transactions for judging bank quality.

Restrictions on the Timing of Offerings

The debt offerings of most, if not all, of the large banks that would be subject to our proposed subordinated-debt requirement should trade frequently in secondary markets. Thus, regulators could make use of those secondary market prices as regulatory tools. But some banks' debt may trade less frequently in secondary markets, if at all. Consequently, market prices on those instruments would provide insufficient information about bank risk. To ensure an adequate flow of regular information about the riskiness of those banks' subordinated-debt offerings, the banks could be required to make regular offerings in the primary market, and the authorities could use those observed primary market yields to gauge bank risk.

We propose, therefore, the following system for regulating subordinated-debt issues. If a bank's qualifying subordinated debt is trading in public secondary markets with adequate minimum and average weekly volumes (measured in dollars of bonds traded) and the prices and yields are adequately observable, then secondary market prices will be deemed adequate as a measure of the market's opinion of the bank's risk. If secondary markets are excessively thin or nonexistent, however, then the issuing bank should be required to come to the primary market regularly.

Banks that are not large enough to see their debt traded in deep secondary markets would face a simple rule, such as that at least 10 percent of their minimum qualifying debt requirement would have to mature in each quarter. The minimum quarterly issuing requirement would permit banks to retain substantial control over the specific timing of issues, while regulators would be able to observe a large enough placement of debt per quarter to ensure an adequate quality of regular price information.

An example helps to clarify how the issuing requirement could be satisfied. Consider a bank with assets of $25 billion, whose subordinated debt does not trade frequently enough in secondary markets. The bank must maintain at least $500 million in outstanding qualifying subordinated debt at all times (2 percent times $25 billion). As any offering's maturity reaches the point of one-year residual maturity, it ceases to qualify for regulatory purposes. Assume for convenience that initial debt maturities are all two years. In the steady state, the bank will have to issue $125 million of debt per quarter. If the bank wished to limit the amount of outstanding subordinated debt to its regulatory minimum, it could regularly redeem outstanding debts with one year of residual maturity by using proceeds of new debt offerings to do so. The bank would thus maintain a constant level of $500 million in outstanding qualifying debt, all of which had residual maturity of greater than one year. Alternatively, the bank could allow all debt issues to mature, a measure that would imply a greater reliance on subordinated debt than is mandated by regulation, as it entails an additional amount of nonqualifying debt (debt with less than one year of residual maturity).

Note that the bank could have chosen instead to satisfy the minimum quarterly issues requirement and the total 2 percent subordinated-debt requirement by issuing $50 million in debt each quarter (which is just equal to 10 percent of its minimum requirement) with initial maturity of ten years. Again, the bank could purchase debts of shorter maturities (including those with residual maturity of greater than one year) by using the proceeds of its new offerings and would thus limit the amount of outstanding debt to $500 million. Therefore, the combination of the 2 percent minimum total subordinated-debt requirement and the 10 percent quarterly issue requirement would still offer banks substantial flexibility in their choice of issuing amounts per quarter and initial maturity. Banks would make that choice by trading off, among other things, the transaction costs, interest costs, and capital structure costs of different issuing strategies.

Capping Permissible Yield Spreads

Thus far we have argued that: (1) subordinated debt should be permitted to count as capital (under the qualifying requirements of section 4); (2) large banks should be required to maintain a minimum of 2 percent of outstanding qualifying subordinated debt relative to their assets; (3) regulators should link market prices of subordinated debt to the structured intervention rules under FDICIA to bolster regulatory discipline with market discipline; and (4) a system for regulating subordinated-debt offerings should be adopted to ensure a regular flow of useful information from the subordinated-debt market.

We also suggest capping the permissible yield on qualifying subordinated debt. We argued above that market discipline may itself "cap" yields on subordinated debt through a form of credit rationing, as in Stiglitz and Weiss (1981). In that case, as a bank's situation deteriorates and the cost of its subordinated debt increases, rationing in the subordinated-debt market forces a shrinkage of outstanding subordinated debt (as it matures), and that shrinkage in turn forces a shrinkage in bank assets or off-balance-sheet commitments (given the minimum 2 percent ratio of subordinated debt to assets and those commitments). Increases in risk that the market is unwilling to bear force banks to shrink their risky assets.

Market discipline, however, does not always result in credit rationing for sufficiently high levels of risk, as it is possible (even within the Stiglitz-Weiss framework) for yield spreads on debt to increase as risk rises. Indeed, the large and growing market for junk debt in recent decades suggests a greater willingness on the part of private debt holders to price risk rather than ration credit to high-risk borrowers. But the desirable risk-reducing aspect of rationing can be replicated to some extent by placing a "junk debt" yield spread ceiling on qualifying subordinated debt.

The following rule would accomplish that objective: Whenever, for three consecutive months, the yield on the qualifying subordinated debt of a bank rises above the yield of moderately risky corporate bonds (say, those rated BBB or Baa) with similar maturity, the bank is considered to be in violation of its subordinated-debt requirement. The bank immediately receives notice to correct the problem, its deposit insurance premium is raised significantly, it is required to submit a plan for restoring market confidence, and it is treated as an undercapitalized bank (as under FDICIA).

By setting a tripwire linking yield spreads to the discipline of the structured early intervention and resolution system, banks are given strong incentives to restore confidence in the market when their yields rise. By using spreads, we ensure flexibility in the measurement of risk; banks will not be penalized for normal cyclical variation in yield spreads. By requiring three consecutive months of high yield spreads to trip the regulatory threshold, we ensure that regulators do not overreact to temporary blips in prices produced by random variations or strategic behavior by competing institutions operating in thin secondary markets.[46]

Can Banks Arbitrage the Subordinated-Debt Requirement?

Some analysts have called attention to the use of on- and off-balance-sheet transactions to arbitrage bank capital requirements. Is our subordinated-debt requirement subject to the same problem? The short answer is no. To the contrary, the subordinated-debt requirement undermines regulatory arbitrage.

Banks would not benefit from moving assets off balance sheet or by creating off-balance-sheet derivatives risks, because the private market (which is often in a superior position to identify the risks of those off-balance-sheet transactions) should incorporate those risks into the pricing of the bank's subordinated debt. Thus, off-balance-sheet transactions that increase risk will be penalized by the market and, if the regulators rely on market signals to measure risk, by the regulators as well.

6
Conclusion

T he Basel standards have proven to be a distorting and, on the whole, ineffectual means of linking minimum capital requirements to bank risk. We have proposed a different approach that focuses on market discipline for large banks to supplement regulatory discipline, as well as to ensure that capital standards are credibly enforced.

The centerpiece of our proposal is a new subordinated-debt requirement, which, along with complementary reforms, would bring market forces to bear in measuring bank risk and rewarding proper bank risk management. Our proposal would provide new information to supervisors and regulators, make the supervisory and regulatory process more effective and accountable, and create a reliable independent mechanism for disciplining bank behavior.

At the same time, it is important to recognize that FDICIA helped to restore a measure of market discipline to banking in the United States by making it more difficult to bail out uninsured depositors and by instituting specific requirements for enforcing violations of bank capital requirements. Those reforms—specifically, prompt corrective action through structured early intervention and resolution—should be adopted by other countries as well. Our proposed subordinated-debt requirement would supplement and strengthen FDICIA while providing strong market-based incentives for banks to disclose more useful information about their risk exposures in a timely fashion.

We urge the adoption of a subordinated-debt requirement, in any of the forms we have outlined, by the Basel Committee and by U.S. regulators. But even if that recommendation is not accepted in its entirety, we have outlined a number of other measures that, singly or ideally in combination, would also strengthen the banking system. Thus, we urge regulators, at minimum, to accept subordinated debt as capital on the same terms as equity, to adopt market-based measures of bank assets and liabilities, and to raise bank capital standards for large banks to something on the order of 10 percent of assets and off-balance-sheet commitments.

The increasing complexity of the financial services business and the growing difficulties regulators and supervisors will face in the coming years in measuring and managing bank risk reinforce the case for acting quickly to update and strengthen prudential bank regulation. We believe that the proposals outlined here would go a long way toward achieving such an important objective.

Appendix

Costs of Equity and Subordinated Debt

D ata on the issuing costs for debt and stock offerings for U.S. corporations, including banks, are reported by Securities Data Co. in its "new issues" database. We collected data on the sum of underwriting fees and other expenses relative to offering proceeds for public common stock issues and subordinated-debt offerings for all large U.S. banks and bank holding companies (those with assets greater than $10 billion) over the period 1995–1999.

We converted the percentage issuing costs for subordinated-debt issues into present values by assuming that the bonds would be rolled over at maturity and that a new bond of the same maturity and yield, with the same issuing cost, would be reissued. We calculated the present value of issuing costs by using the yield on the bonds at the date of their offering to discount the future.

The present value of issuing costs for bank subordinated-debt offerings sold to the public averaged 1.53 percent of offerings. The average issuing cost for common stock offerings sold to the public for the same sample of banks was 3.46 percent. Thus, the transaction costs of subordinated-debt offerings are less than half those of common stock offerings for large U.S. banks.

Notes

1. *Capital* is often defined as the net worth of an institution. As we discuss below, however, the definition of the term is more complex.

2. The Basel Committee has suggested that emerging market economies adopt its minimum capital standards, suitably increased to account for the greater volatility in asset values that those countries tend to experience. In this monograph, however, we consider only capital requirements for large banks in developed countries. For an analysis of problems besetting banks in other economies, see Goldstein (1997), Benston (1999a), and Calomiris (1999).

3. For a more detailed discussion, see Jensen and Meckling (1976), Myers (1977), and James (1988).

4. See Kaufman (1994).

5. For a more detailed discussion, see Gorton and Pennacchi (1990), Calomiris and Kahn (1991), and Diamond and Rajan (1999).

6. See Kaufman (1994), Calomiris and Mason (1997), and Calomiris and Wilson (1998).

7. See Benston (1995) and Benston and Kaufman (1998).

8. This analysis assumes that the deposit is paid in full at the time of bank failure. Although that is true in the United States, it is not the case in all countries. See Kaufman and Seelig (2000).

9. Moral hazard is a problem common to all insurance arrangements, since by purchasing the insurance, policy holders have reduced incentives to avoid the events that might trigger the payment of claims. In the private insur-

ance market, insurers attempt to offset that problem with deductibles, risk-related premiums, and other measures. Capital standards for banks can be viewed as the equivalent of a deductible for the federal government that provides the insurance through the Federal Deposit Insurance Corporation.

10. See Calomiris (1990, 1992).

11. See Barth, Brumbaugh, and Litan (1992) and Kaufman (1995).

12. See Kane (1989), Barth (1991), and Benston and Kaufman (1990).

13. The two most significant pieces of legislation were the Riegle-Neal Interstate Banking Act of 1994 and the Gramm-Leach-Bliley Financial Modernization Act of 1999.

14. See Benston (1985) and Barth (1991).

15. FDICIA largely adopted the structured early intervention and resolution procedures first proposed by Benston and Kaufman (1988) and expanded and endorsed by the Shadow Financial Regulatory Committee (1989). See also Benston et al. (1989), who also advanced an alternative proposal that banks be required to fully collateralize their deposits with safe, liquid securities.

16. The details of this system are more fully explained in section 4.

17. See Benston and Kaufman (1998).

18. See Benink and Benston (1999).

19. See Lindgren, Garcia, and Saal (1996), International Monetary Fund (1998), Caprio and Klingabiel (2000), and Kaufman (2000).

20. See Goldstein (1997).

21. See Benston (1992b) for a more extended criticism.

22. Cantor and Packer (1994) claim that the use of private ratings in setting risk standards in securitizations has produced something of a race to the bottom in private ratings of those instruments in the United States. See also Shadow Financial Regulatory Committee (1998) and Partnoy (1999). Argentina also has experienced related

problems in its use of private ratings. See Calomiris and Powell (2000).

23. Indeed, even the ratings agencies have raised these objections. See Kraus (2000).

24. See Basel Committee on Banking Supervision (2000).

25. See Benston (1992a).

26. See Benston (1982) for a description and an analysis of the divergences between accounting numbers and market values.

27. The Federal Reserve Board agrees that securities in which a bank trades should be stated at market values, but it opposes the Financial Accounting Standards Board's proposals to include the market values of all derivatives in banks' primary financial statements, primarily because "fair value estimation techniques (particularly for derivatives) are not yet sufficiently robust to be relied upon exclusively in financial statements" (Phillips 1997). Rather, the Fed favors "placing market values in meaningful supplemental disclosures" (ibid.). We suggest that those market values be included in the measurement of capital for regulatory purposes. Although they may not be perfect, they are likely to be more meaningful than historical cost. With respect to derivatives, we favor permitting banks to offset unrealized gains or losses on hedged assets and liabilities with realized losses and gains on hedging derivatives, an approach similar to the one adopted by the Financial Accounting Standards Board in Financial Statement 133 (1998). See Benston (1997) for details.

28. See Benston (1989) for an additional discussion.

29. The problems of measuring capital in less-developed economies often are much more difficult. Attesting public accountants in developing countries may be less experienced and less reliable. More important, stockholders can avoid, and in developing countries sometimes have avoided, capital requirements by borrowing funds from their banks, directly and often indirectly, to "invest" in their banks' capital. See Benston (1999a) for a more detailed explana-

tion and for steps that banking authorities can take to control such fraud.

30. See Kaufman (1992).

31. The precise technique for computing the amounts of off-balance-sheet commitments is not as important under our proposed subordinated-debt requirement (discussed below) as under the current Basel standards. That is so because our proposal harnesses market forces directly to discipline inappropriate off-balance-sheet risks.

32. As discussed later, we suggest requiring large banks to issue an amount equal to at least 2 percent of their total on- and off-balance-sheet assets in the form of subordinated debt.

33. See Calomiris and Himmelberg (1999).

34. Some preferred stock carries a contract-like obligation to make dividend payments, if not in the current period, then in subsequent periods if dividend payments are missed. Such a feature makes the dividend right "cumulative."

35. The literature outlining the merits of a subordinated-debt requirement includes Horvitz (1983, 1984), Baer and Brewer (1986), Benston et al. (1986), Benston and Kaufman (1988), Keehn (1989), Shadow Financial Regulatory Committee (1989), Wall (1989), Benston (1992b, 1999b), Herring and Litan (1995), Calomiris (1997, 1999), Litan and Rauch (1997), Board of Governors of the Federal Reserve System (1999), and Calomiris and Litan (2000). The empirical literature showing that subordinated-debt prices, in practice, provide useful information about bank risk includes Benston (1994), Flannery (1998), Berger, Davies, and Flannery (1998), Jagtiani, Kaufman, and Lemieux (1999), and Morgan and Stiroh (1999).

36. It is important to bear in mind that equity price changes do not provide clear signals about bank risk. For example, as bank net worth falls, increases in asset risk will produce increases in equity values for banks with low or negative net worth, particularly if those banks are insured. For empirical evidence, see Brewer (1995).

37. For details, see Benston and Kaufman (1988).

38. This feature responds to arguments made by Diamond and Rajan (1999). Specifically, they argue that it may be beneficial to prevent uninsured debt holders from being able to renegotiate debt contracts in states of the world where the banks' prospects have deteriorated. By requiring that old debt can only be purchased with the proceeds of new debt issues, we avoid that problem.

39. Banks could try to circumvent the intent of the subordinated-debt requirement by entering into swap transactions with holders of the debt. To forestall that possibility, regulators could require reporting of all such transactions and prohibit their use as part of the normal supervisory process.

40. See Shadow Financial Regulatory Committee (1989).

41. This calculation is based on data provided in Board of Governors of the Federal Reserve System (1999).

42. We have offered all of our proposals in this monograph—including the subordinated-debt requirement—only for very large banks. Requiring smaller banks to issue subordinated debt could be costly, since many may find it very hard to place debt publicly. Still, it is likely that some smaller banks could use less-expensive private placements of debt as an alternative to public offerings. The private purchasers could act as outside monitors of the operations of the banks. Indeed, historically, small banks maintained correspondent relationships and other interbank lending arrangements with large banks that entailed precisely that kind of monitoring and lending (Calomiris and Mason 1997). In the absence of better evidence on the issuing costs of private placements of subordinated debt for small banks, however, the Shadow Financial Regulatory Committee believes that it is best to exempt them from the subordinated-debt requirement, at least initially.

43. See, for example, Shadow Financial Regulatory Committee (1997a, 1997b).

44. Even the Federal Reserve staff study recognizes the

conceptual arguments in favor of imposing the requirement at the bank level, although the study sides with a
requirement at the holding company level for "practical
reasons" (Board of Governors of the Federal Reserve System 1999, 30).

45. See Calomiris and Gorton (1991), Calomiris and
Kahn (1991), and Calomiris and Mason (1997).

46. See Garber (1999).

References

Altman, Edward I., and Anthony Saunders. 1999. "The BIS Proposal on Capital Adequacy and Ratings: A Commentary." Working paper, Stern School of Business, New York University, November.

Baer, Herbert, and Elijah Brewer III. 1986. "Uninsured Deposits as a Source of Market Discipline: Some New Evidence." *Federal Reserve Bank of Chicago Economic Perspectives* (September/October): 23–31.

Barth, James R. 1991. *The Great Savings and Loan Debacle.* Washington, D.C.: AEI Press.

Barth, James R., R. Dan Brumbaugh, and Robert E. Litan. 1992. *The Future of American Banking.* New York: W. E. Sharpe.

Basel Committee on Banking Supervision. 2000. "Range of Practice in Banks' Internal Ratings Systems." January.

Benink, Harald, and George J. Benston. 1999. "The Future of Banking Regulation in Developed Countries: Lessons from and for Europe." Working paper, Emory University, June.

Benston, George J. 1982. "Accounting Numbers and Economic Values." *Antitrust Bulletin* 27 (Spring): 161–215.

———. 1985. *An Analysis of the Causes of Savings and Loan Failures.* Monograph Series in Finance and Economics, Salomon Center, Stern School of Business, New York University, Monograph 1985-4/5.

———. 1989. "Market-Value Accounting: Benefits, Costs and Incentives." In *Proceedings: A Conference on Bank*

Structure and Competition. Chicago: Federal Reserve Bank of Chicago, 547–69.

———. 1992a. "The Purpose of Capital for Institutions with Government-Insured Deposits." *Journal of Financial Services Research* 5: 369–84.

———. 1992b. "International Bank Capital Standards." In *Emerging Challenges for the International Financial Services Industry,* edited by James R. Barth and Phillip F. Bartholomew. *Research in International Business and Finance* 9. Greenwich, Conn.: JAI Press.

———. 1994. "Market Discipline: The Role of Uninsured Depositors and Other Market Participants." In *Safeguarding the Banking System in an Environment of Financial Cycles,* edited by Richard E. Randall. Federal Reserve Bank of Boston Conference Series No. 37. Boston: Federal Reserve Bank of Boston, 65–95.

———. 1995. "Safety Nets and Moral Hazard in Banking." In *Financial Stability in a Changing Environment,* edited by Kuniho Sawamoto, Zenata Nakajima, and Hiroo Taguchi. New York: St. Martin's Press, 329–77.

———. 1997. "Accounting for Derivatives: Back to Basics." *Journal of Applied Corporate Finance* 10 (Fall): 46–58.

———. 1999a. "Banking Fragility, Effectiveness, and Regulation in Less-Developed Countries." In *Asia: An Analysis of Financial Crisis,* edited by William C. Hunter, George G. Kaufman, and Thomas H. Krueger. Norwell, Mass.: Kluwer Academic Publishers, 269–89.

———. 1999b. *Regulating Financial Markets: A Critique and Some Proposals.* Washington, D.C.: American Enterprise Institute.

Benston, George J., and George G. Kaufman. 1988. *Risk and Solvency Regulation of Depository Institutions: Past Policies and Current Options.* Monograph Series in Finance and Economics, Salomon Center, Stern School of Business, New York University, Monograph 1988-1.

————. 1990. "Understanding the Savings and Loan Debacle." *Public Interest* 99 (Spring): 79–95.

————. 1998. "Deposit Insurance Reform in the FDIC Improvement Act: The Experience to Date." *Federal Reserve Bank of Chicago Economic Perspectives* (March/April): 2–20.

Benston, George J., R. Dan Brumbaugh, Jr., Jack M. Guttentag, Richard J. Herring, George G. Kaufman, Robert E. Litan, and Kenneth E. Scott. 1989. *Blueprint for Restructuring America's Financial Institutions.* Washington, D.C.: Brookings Institution.

Benston, George J., Robert A. Eisenbeis, Paul M. Horvitz, Edward J. Kane, and George G. Kaufman. 1986. *Perspectives on Safe and Sound Banking.* Cambridge: MIT Press.

Berger, Allen N., Sally M. Davies, and Mark J. Flannery. 1998. "Comparing Market and Regulatory Assessments of Bank Performance: Who Knows What When?" Working paper, Federal Reserve Board, March.

Board of Governors of the Federal Reserve System. 1999. "Using Subordinated Debt as an Instrument of Market Discipline." Staff Study 172, December.

Brewer, Elijah, III. 1985. "The Impact of Current Deposit Insurance on S&L Shareholders' Risk/Return Tradeoffs." *Journal of Financial Services Research* 9: 65–69.

Calomiris, Charles W. 1990. "Is Deposit Insurance Necessary? An Historical Perspective." *Journal of Economic History* 50 (June): 283–95.

————. 1992. "Do Vulnerable Economies Need Deposit Insurance? Lessons from the U.S. Agricultural Boom and Bust in the 1920s." In *If Texas Were Chile: A Primer on Banking Reform,* edited by Philip Brock. San Francisco: ICS Press, 237–314.

————. 1997. *The Postmodern Bank Safety Net.* Washington, D.C.: AEI Press.

———. 1999. "Building an Incentive-Compatible Safety Net." *Journal of Banking and Finance* 23 (October): 1499–520.

Calomiris, Charles W., and Gary Gorton. 1991. "The Origins of Banking Panics: Models, Facts, and Bank Regulation." In *Financial Markets and Financial Crises*, edited by R. Glenn Hubbard. Chicago: University of Chicago Press, 109–73.

Calomiris, Charles W., and Charles P. Himmelberg. 1999. "Investment Banking Costs as a Measure of the Cost of Access to External Finance." Working paper, Columbia University Graduate School of Business, September.

Calomiris, Charles W., and Charles M. Kahn. 1991. "The Role of Demandable Debt in Structuring Optimal Banking Arrangements." *American Economic Review* 81 (June): 497–513.

Calomiris, Charles W., and Robert E. Litan. 2000. "Financial Regulation in a Global Marketplace." Brookings-Wharton Papers on Financial Services 3, forthcoming.

Calomiris, Charles W., and Joseph R. Mason. 1997. "Contagion and Bank Failures during the Great Depression: The June 1932 Chicago Banking Panic." *American Economic Review* 87 (December): 863–83.

Calomiris, Charles W., and Andrew Powell. 2000. "Can Emerging Market Bank Regulators Establish Credible Discipline? The Case of Argentina, 1992–1999." In *Prudential Supervision: What Works and What Doesn't*, edited by Frederic S. Mishkin. Chicago: University of Chicago Press, forthcoming.

Calomiris, Charles W., and Berry Wilson. 1998. "Bank Capital and Portfolio Management: The 1930s Capital Crunch and Scramble to Shed Risk." National Bureau of Economic Research Working Paper No. 6649, July.

Cantor, Richard, and Frank Packer. 1994. "The Credit Rating Industry." *Federal Reserve Bank of New York Quarterly Review* (Summer/Fall): 1–26.

Caprio, Gerard, and Daniela Klingabiel. 2000. "Bank Insolvency: Bad Luck, Bad Policy, or Bad Banking?" In *Modernizing Financial Systems,* edited by Dimitri Papadimitriou. New York: St. Martin's Press: 267–301.

Diamond, Douglas, and Raghuram G. Rajan. 1999. "Liquidity Risk, Liquidity Creation and Financial Fragility: A Theory of Banking." National Bureau of Economic Research Working Paper No. 7430, December.

Financial Accounting Standards Board. 1998. "Accounting for Derivative Instruments and Hedging." Statement No. 133, June.

Flannery, Mark. 1998. "Using Market Information in Prudential Bank Supervision: A Review of the U.S. Empirical Evidence." *Journal of Money, Credit, and Banking* 30: 273–305.

Garber, Peter. 1999. "Notes on Market-Based Bank Regulation." Working paper, Deutsche Bank, December.

Goldstein, Morris. 1997. *The Case for an International Banking Standard.* Washington, D.C.: Institute for International Economics.

Gorton, Gary, and George Pennacchi. 1990. "Financial Intermediaries and Liquidity Creation." *Journal of Finance* 45 (March): 49–71.

Herring, Richard J., and Robert E. Litan. 1995. *Financial Regulation in the Global Economy.* Washington, D.C.: Brookings Institution.

Horvitz, Paul. 1983. "Market Discipline Is Best Provided by Subordinated Creditors." *American Banker,* July 15.

———. 1984. "Subordinated Debt Is Key to New Bank Capital Requirements." *American Banker,* December 31.

International Monetary Fund. 1998. *World Economic Outlook.* Washington, D.C.: International Monetary Fund, May.

Jagtiani, Julapa, George G. Kaufman, and Catharine Lemieux. 1999. "Do Markets Discipline Banks and Bank Holding Companies? Evidence from Debt Pricing." Working paper, Federal Reserve Bank of Chicago, May.

James, Christopher. 1988. "The Use of Loan Sales and Standby Letters of Credit by Commercial Banks." *Journal of Monetary Economics* 22 (November): 395–422.

Jensen, Michael C., and William H. Meckling. 1976. "Theory of the Firm: Managerial Behavior, Agency Costs, and Ownership Structure." *Journal of Financial Economics* 3: 305–60.

Kane, Edward J. 1989. *The S&L Insurance Mess: How Did It Happen?* Washington, D.C.: Urban Institute Press.

Kaufman, George G. 1992. "Capital in Banking: Past, Present, and Future." *Journal of Financial Services Research* 5: 385–402.

———. 1994. "Bank Contagion: A Review of the Theory and Evidence." *Journal of Financial Services Research* 8: 123–50.

———. 1995. "The U.S. Banking Debacle of the 1980s." *Financier* (May): 9–26.

———. 2000. "Banking and Currency Crises and Systemic Risk: A Taxonomy and Review." *Financial Markets, Institutions, and Instruments*, forthcoming.

Kaufman, George G., and Steven A. Seelig. 2000. "Treatment of Depositors at Failed Banks and the Cost and Severity of Banking Crisis." Working paper, Loyola University, Chicago, January.

Keehn, Silas. 1989. "Banking on the Balance: Powers and the Safety Net, A Proposal." Federal Reserve Bank of Chicago.

Kraus, James R. 2000. "Rating Agencies Side with Banks on Risk Management Issue." *American Banker,* January 20, 5.

Kwast, Myron, and Wayne Passmore. 1997. "The Subsidy Provided by the Federal Safety Net: Theory, Measurement, and Containment." Federal Reserve Board Working Paper 1997-58, December.

Lindgren, Carl-Johan, Gillian Garcia, and Matthew L. Saal. 1996. *Bank Soundness and Macroeconomic Policy.* Washington, D.C.: International Monetary Fund.

Litan, Robert E., and Jonathan Rauch. 1997. "American Finance for the 21st Century." U.S. Treasury Department, November.

Morgan, Donald P., and Kevin J. Stiroh. 1999. "Can Bond Holders Discipline Banks?" Working paper, Federal Reserve Bank of New York, August.

Myers, Stewart C. 1977. "Determinants of Corporate Borrowing." *Journal of Financial Economics* 5: 147–75.

Partnoy, Frank. 1999. "The Siskel and Ebert of Financial Markets? Two Thumbs Down for the Credit Rating Agencies." *Washington University Law Quarterly* 77: 619–712.

Phillips, Susan M. 1997. "Testimony before the Subcommittee on Capital Markets, Securities, and Government-Sponsored Enterprises of the Committee on Banking and Financial Services." U.S. House of Representatives, October 1.

Scott, Hal S., and Shinsaku Iwahara. 1994. "In Search of a Level Playing Field: The Implementation of the Basel Accord in Japan and the United States." Occasional Paper No. 46. Washington, D.C.: Group of Thirty.

Shadow Financial Regulatory Committee. 1989. "Statement No. 41: An Outline of a Program for Deposit Insurance and Regulatory Reform." February 13. Published in *Journal of Financial Services Research* 6 (August 1992), Supplement: 78–82.

———. 1997a. "Statement No. 139: H.R. 10 ('Leach Bill') and the Commerce Subcommittee Draft." September 22. Published in *Journal of Financial Services Research* 13 (April 1998): 171–72.

———. 1997b. "Statement No. 142: Congress and Financial Reform." December 7. Published in *Journal of Financial Services Research* 13 (June 1998): 321–22.

———. 1998. "Statement No. 149: The Use of Private Credit Ratings for Determining Capital Requirements for Securitizations." Published in *Journal of Financial Services Research* 14 (December 1998): 228.

Stiglitz, Joseph E., and Andrew Weiss. 1981. "Credit Rationing in Markets with Imperfect Information." *American Economic Review* 71 (June): 393–410.

Wall, Larry D. 1989. "A Plan for Reducing Future Deposit Insurance Losses: Puttable Subordinated Debt." *Federal Reserve Bank of Atlanta Economic Review* (July/August): 2–17.

About the Authors

RICHARD C. ASPINWALL is an independent economic adviser, dealing primarily with not-for-profit organizations. Before his retirement, he was chief economist at the Chase Manhattan Bank.

GEORGE J. BENSTON is the John H. Harland Professor of Finance, Accounting, and Economics at the Goizueta Business School and professor of economics in the College of Arts and Sciences at Emory University. He is the author of *Regulating Financial Markets: A Critique and Some Proposals* (AEI Press, 1999).

CHARLES W. CALOMIRIS is the Paul M. Montrone Professor of Finance and Economics at the Columbia University Graduate School of Business and a professor in the Department of International and Public Affairs at Columbia's School of International and Public Affairs. The codirector of AEI's Financial Deregulation Project, he is also a research associate of the National Bureau of Economic Research.

FRANKLIN R. EDWARDS is the Arthur F. Burns Professor of Economics and Finance at the Columbia University Graduate School of Business and chairman of the Finance and Economics Division. His areas of interest include financial economics and banking, derivatives, and securities markets.

SCOTT E. HARRINGTON is professor of insurance and finance and the Francis Hipp Distinguished Faculty Fellow at the

Darla Moore School of Business of the University of South Carolina. Mr. Harrington is an expert on the economics of insurance markets and insurance regulation.

RICHARD J. HERRING is the Jacob Safra Professor of International Banking and professor of finance at the Wharton School of the University of Pennsylvania, where he is currently vice dean and director of the undergraduate division. His research interests include international finance and international aspects of financial regulation.

PAUL M. HORVITZ is professor of finance at the University of Houston. Previously, he was director of research and deputy to the chairman of the Federal Deposit Insurance Corporation.

GEORGE G. KAUFMAN is the John F. Smith Professor of Finance and Economics at Loyola University, Chicago. Previously, he was an economist at the Federal Reserve Bank of Chicago (where he remains a consultant), served as deputy to the assistant secretary of the U.S. Department of the Treasury, and taught at a number of other universities, including the University of Oregon, Stanford University, and the University of California at Berkeley. He is cochairman of the Shadow Financial Regulatory Committee.

ROBERT E. LITAN is vice president and director of the Economic Studies Program at the Brookings Institution, where he also holds the Cabot Family Chair in Economics. He is cochairman of the Shadow Financial Regulatory Committee.

ROBERTA ROMANO is the Allen Duffy/Class of 1960 Professor of Law at the Yale Law School. She is a fellow of the American Academy of Arts and Sciences and a research associate of the National Bureau of Economic Research and was president of the American Law and Economics Association in 1998–1999.

HAL S. SCOTT is the Nomura Professor and director of the Program on International Financial Systems at Harvard Law School. He is the coauthor of the textbook *International Finance, Transactions, Policy, and Regulation* (Foundation Press, 1999), now in its 6th edition.

KENNETH E. SCOTT is the Parsons Professor Emeritus of Law and Business at Stanford Law School, where he has been on the faculty since 1967. Before that, he was in private practice in New York and held positions in the state and federal governments in California and Washington, D.C.

PETER J. WALLISON is a resident fellow at the American Enterprise Institute. An attorney specializing in corporate and financial law, he is the codirector of AEI's Financial Deregulation Project.

www.ingramcontent.com/pod-product-compliance
Lightning Source LLC
Jackson TN
JSHW011941131224
75386JS00041B/1502